W9-BAT-438

Congress

Katherine Krieg

rourkeeducationalmedia.com

*Scan for Related Titles
and Teacher Resources*

Before Reading:

Building Academic Vocabulary and Background Knowledge

Before reading a book, it is important to tap into what your child or students already know about the topic. This will help them develop their vocabulary, increase their reading comprehension, and make connections across the curriculum.

1. *Look at the cover of the book. What will this book be about?*
2. *What do you already know about the topic?*
3. *Let's study the Table of Contents. What will you learn about in the book's chapters?*
4. *What would you like to learn about this topic? Do you think you might learn about it from this book? Why or why not?*
5. *Use a reading journal to write about your knowledge of this topic. Record what you already know about the topic and what you hope to learn about the topic.*
6. *Read the book.*
7. *In your reading journal, record what you learned about the topic and your response to the book.*
8. *After reading the book complete the activities below.*

Content Area Vocabulary
Read the list. What do these words mean?

approve
bill
budget
Capitol
elected
election
impeach
majority
population
represent
tax
veto

After Reading:

Comprehension and Extension Activity

After reading the book, work on the following questions with your child or students in order to check their level of reading comprehension and content mastery.

1. *What does impeach mean? (Summarize)*
2. *Why must a representative live in the state they want to represent? (Asking questions)*
3. *Who are your state congressmen? (Text to self connection)*
4. *What are the duties of Congress? (Summarize)*
5. *Explain how many representatives and senators each state gets. (Summarize)*

Extension Activity

Chose three states, with one being your own. Research the state size, population, and number of representatives. Create a bar graph that depicts this information. What conclusions can you draw from the state's size and population? The population and the number of representatives? The size of the state and the number of representatives?

Table of Contents

The U.S. Congress is an important part of the government in the United States. It is the only part of the government that is completely chosen by the people.

Members of Congress pose for a photo at the U.S. Capitol building.

Congress is made up of the U.S. House of Representatives and the U.S. Senate. There are 535 members in Congress.

In 2013, 98 women served in the U.S. Congress. More congressional seats were held by women than ever before.

Congressional floor of the U.S. Congress.

Congress is the legislative branch of government. Its main job is to make laws. But it has other jobs too.

The idea for the U.S. Congress was formed in 1787.

Congress meets in a room called the House Chamber in the Capitol building.

Congress meets several times throughout the year. Meetings are held in the **Capitol** building in Washington, D.C.

★ The House of Representatives ★

The House of Representatives is called the House for short. There are 435 representatives in the House. Each member is there to **represent** his or her state.

A representative is also called a congressman or congresswoman.

When Congress meets, they fill the House Chamber.

Some states have only one House representative. But many have more than one. The number of representatives per state is based on that state's **population**. The more people living in the state, the more representatives the state has in the House.

In 2013, California had the most representatives with 53. The number of representatives can change as populations change.

John Boehner is the Speaker of the House of Representatives. The speaker is the leader of the House sessions and gives representatives permission to speak or debate important government issues.

345

CAUCUS ROOM

Representatives must live in the state they want to represent. Representatives are **elected** every two years. Only the people living in their state can vote for them.

Citizens vote for who they would like to represent their state.

Some non-states also have representatives in the House. These include the District of Columbia, Puerto Rico, the Virgin Islands, Guam, American Samoa, and the Commonwealth of the Northern Mariana Islands. However, though they may speak on behalf of the people in their districts, these representatives are not permitted to vote on new laws.

Puerto Rico's representative, Pedro Pierluisi, may debate new laws in Congress, but is not permitted to vote.

The Senate

The other part of Congress is the U.S. Senate. The Senate is made up of 100 people. They are called senators.

Hillary Clinton was the first former First Lady to become a senator.

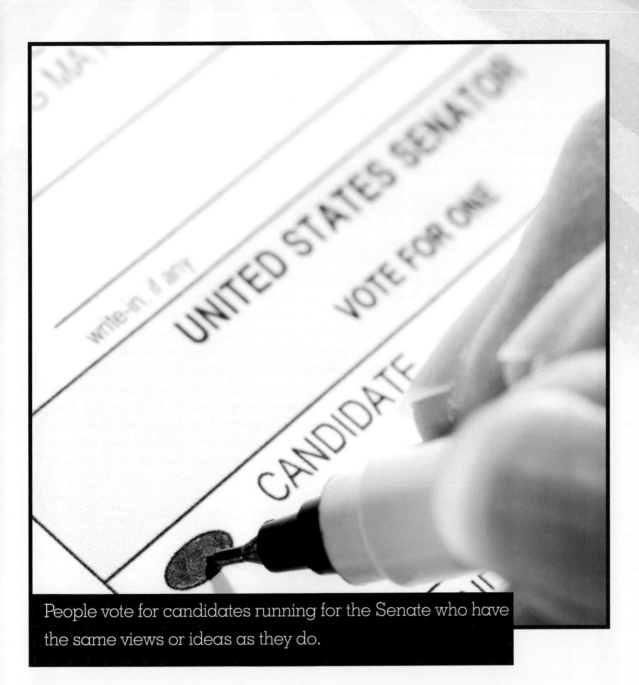

People vote for candidates running for the Senate who have the same views or ideas as they do.

Each state elects two senators. The population of the state is not taken into account. With each state having the same number of senators, a sparsely populated state like North Dakota has the same power as a highly populated state like California.

Senators are elected every six years. But not all states elect senators in the same year. The states are grouped into three classes. Each class elects senators during a different **election** year.

Senators can represent more than one state in their lifetime if they move around. Senator James Shield (1878–1920) is the only person to have represented three states: Illinois, Minnesota, and Missouri.

Classes in Each U.S. State

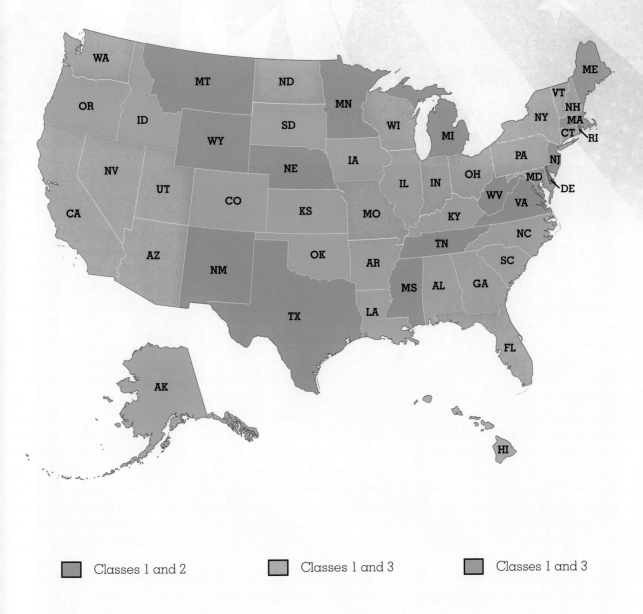

Classes 1 and 2   Classes 1 and 3   Classes 1 and 3

Each state belongs to two classes, one for each senator.

Congress at Work

Together, the House of Representatives and the Senate form Congress. The main job of Congress is to **approve** laws. Congress has other responsibilities too.

Every year the president delivers the State of the Union Address in front of Congress.

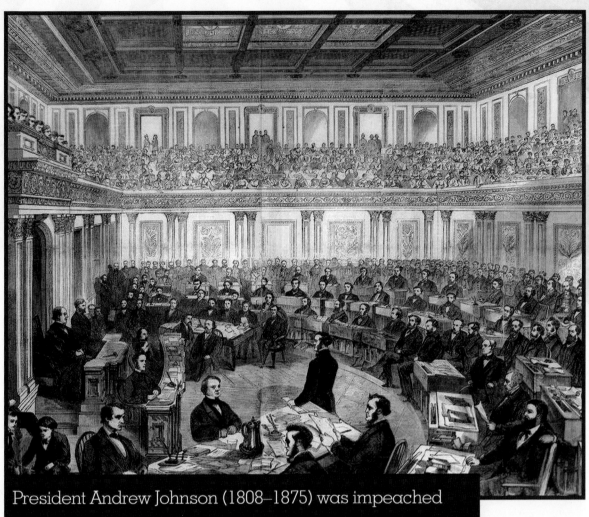

President Andrew Johnson (1808–1875) was impeached in 1868, but he remained president.

Congress makes the government's **budget** each year. It works to decide how much **tax** U.S. citizens will pay each year.

One big responsibility of Congress is its power to declare war. Though the president commands the U.S. military, only Congress can declare war on other countries. Congress can also **impeach** a president if he or she does something that is against the law or U.S. Constitution.

Usually, Congress is focused on lawmaking. A law starts out as a **bill**. The bill is brought to Congress. The House and the Senate each have a chance to **debate** the bill.

Anyone can write a bill, but a member of Congress is the only person who can bring the bill to debate.

George Washington, the first president of the United States, didn't think that Congress should add many laws.

After debating its pros and cons, Congress will vote on the bill. The bill only passes if it gets the **majority** of the votes in both the House and the Senate. But, before the bill becomes a law, the president must approve it.

When the president does not approve a bill from Congress, it is called a **veto**.

A Voice

The United States is a large country with many people. People have different ideas about what is important. They might disagree about what laws should be created.

People often make signs for rallies to express their support for or against certain laws.

U.S. citizens can elect representatives and senators who share their views. This way, citizens can have a voice in the

Glossary

approve (uh-PROOV): to accept a plan or idea

bill (bil): a plan for a new law

budget (BUHJ-it): a plan for how much money will be earned and spent

Capitol (KAP-i-tuhl): the building in which the legislative body meets

elected (i-LEKT-ed): to be picked through a vote

election (i-LEK-shuhn): an event when people vote to choose someone for a job or position

impeach (im-PEECH): to charge someone with committing a crime that can result in he or she being removed from a political position

majority (muh-JOR-i-tee): more than half of a group

population (pahp-yuh-LAY-shuhn): the number of people living in a specific area

represent (rep-ri-ZENT): to speak or act on behalf of others

tax (TAKS): money people pay to the government to support it

veto (VEE-toh): to reject a bill

Index

Show What You Know

1. Who makes up the U.S. Congress?
2. How many representatives are in the House? How often are they elected?
3. Why might some representatives not be permitted to vote?
4. Why did the author share the number of female representatives?
5. What role does Congress have in creating laws?

Websites to Visit

kids.clerk.house.gov/grade-school/lesson.html?intID=17
www.congressforkids.net/
www.ducksters.com/history/us_legislative_branch.php

About the Author

Katherine Krieg is author of many books for young people. Katherine demonstrates her rights as a U.S. citizen by voting in every election.

Meet The Author!
www.meetREMauthors.com

© 2015 Rourke Educational Media

All rights reserved. No part of this book may be reproduced or utilized in any form or by any means, electronic or mechanical including photocopying, recording, or by any information storage and retrieval system without permission in writing from the publisher.

www.rourkeeducationalmedia.com

PHOTO CREDITS: Cover © Dan Thornberg, whitehouse.gov; Title Page, page 8 © whitehouse.gov; page 4 © 2010 Getty Images; page 5 © Brendan Hoffman; page 6 © Chip Somodevilla; page 7 © Songquan Deng; page 9 © Win McNamee; page 10 © Patrick Herrera; page 11 © GDA/EL Nuevo Dia/Puerto Rico/ AP Images; page 12 © Visions of America LLC; page 13 © YinYang; page 14, 18 © Library of Congress; page 15 © GuiTAG; page 16 © Chuck Kennedy; page 17 © Wikipedia/ Theodore R. Davis; page 19 © Pete Souza; page 20 © wh1600; page 21 © Dieter Spears/Inhaus Creative

Edited by: Jill Sherman

Cover by: Nicola Stratford, nicolastratford.com
Interior design by: Jen Thomas

Library of Congress PCN Data

Congress/ Katherine Krieg
 (U.S. Government and Civics)
  ISBN 978-1-62717-679-8 (hard cover)
  ISBN 978-1-62717-801-3 (soft cover)
  ISBN 978-1-62717-917-1 (e-Book)
Library of Congress Control Number: 2014935454

Printed in the United States of America, North Mankato, Minnesota

Also Available as: